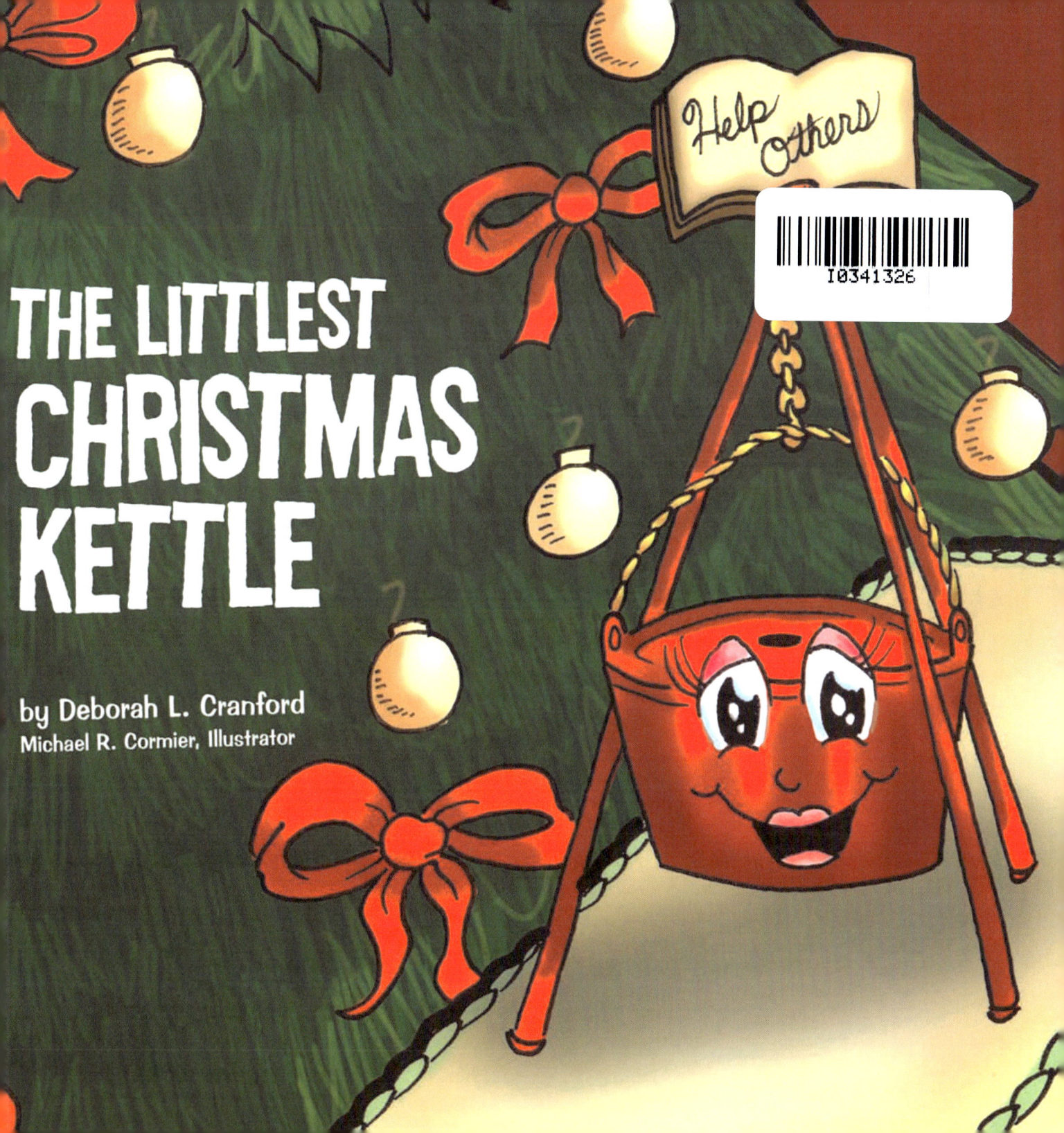

THE LITTLEST CHRISTMAS KETTLE

by Deborah L. Cranford
Michael R. Cormier, Illustrator

Copyright 2012 by **Deborah L. Kunkle Cranford**

All rights reserved. No portion of this book may be reproduced, stored in a retrieval system, or transmitted in any form or by any means – electronic, mechanical, photocopy, recording, scanning, or other – except for brief quotations in critical reviews or articles, without the prior written permission of the author.

Reprinted in 2025 by Book Launch USA

ISBN: 978-1-4003-8884-4

Whoever is kind to the needy honors God

Proverbs 14:31 NIV

For the wonderful stories she told me when I was a child,

this is dedicated to my mother,

Loah Louise Richie Kunle;

and to my loving husband Paul,

and our three precocious children

for their great expectations and unwavering support.

GREETINGS

It would take the creative talent of (Major) Debbi Cranford to unearth lessons from the icon of The Salvation Army's appeal at Christmas time: the red kettle.

This is a delightful tale that will especially capture the imaginations of children who will become the donors and volunteers of the future.

But *The Littlest Christmas Kettle* also holds an abundance of lessons for every adult, such as the joy of working in community to achieve a great purpose. In charming fashion, (Major) Debbi presents the matter of giving through service in a way that will leave readers convinced that such imaginings can come true-a narrative that is urgently needed for such a time as this in our nation.

And I have a feeling that Sallie Kettle has more to reveal to us. So Major Cranford, please: Write on!

Commissioner Israel L. Gaither

The Salvation Army

USA National Commander, Retired

A NOTE FROM THE AUTHOR

The Salvation Army is well known in the United States for its method of using red kettles to raise funds to help needy families during the Christmas season.

What follows is a fictional story that employs that tradition in a fanciful manner.

The author trusts that readers who may be unfamiliar with Salvation Army terms, such as officer/Major (pastor), corps (church), and Christmas kettle effort (fund-raising), will not miss the message that the idea to help others can begin with the smallest among us, and can produce aid in great quantities when such an effort is joined by many.

To make a donation to The Salvation Army
Christmas program in your area,
please call your local
Salvation Army.

CHAPTER 1
SALLIE IS RESCUED

Anna heard quiet sobs coming from the big wooden bin. She and her father had gone to the basement of the corps to gather Christmas kettles from the storage bin. At first, the sniffling sound was faint; Anna could barely hear it. But as her father took out each large red kettle, the crying seemed to grow louder and louder.

Full of curiosity, Anna leaned on tippy-toes to look closely into the bin. Even though she was tall for a soon- to-be six-year-old, she had to stretch to see. There, tucked far into a dark corner, was a small red kettle with tears streaming down its face.

"What's wrong, little bucket?" asked Anna. Her voice caused the little kettle to jump, making a noisy clatter against the sides of the bin.

Recovering from the scare, the kettle answered, "I'm sad and lonely. Every year I'm left here by myself. The other kettles and I sleep most of the year, but at Christmas time, all the big kettles get to go outside. I'm so small no one ever sees me and I just fall asleep again."

Between sniffles, the kettle continued. "My family comes back on Christmas Eve with wonderful stories of shoppers dropping in their coins, and sometimes even dollar bills, so that poor children will have a nice Christmas. I never get to help," sighed the littlest kettle. "It sounds like so much fun, and all I get to do is snooze until all the other kettles come back to this bin."

"Daddy, that little bucket wants to help, too," Anna said, pointing to the far right-hand corner. She leaned in again and asked, "What's your name, little bucket?" "My name is Sallie," responded the little red kettle.

Anna turned to her father and asked, "Does Sallie have to stay in that bin again this Christmas, Daddy? She seems so sad and she'll be all by herself."

"How do you know she's sad and lonely, Anna? And what a cute name you've given her."

"Daaaddy, she just told me her name is Sallie, and she doesn't want to miss another Christmas!"

"Let's have a look at her. You said her name is Sallie?" He leaned over the edge of the bin, stretched his arm into the dark corner, and picked up Sallie by her lopsided handle. He rested her on the edge of the bin to get a good look at the little kettle.

"The handle is broken and the paint is chipped and faded. I don't think I have time to fix her before we put the other kettles at the stores, and she's too small for the big stands we use with the big kettles. I'm not sure what we could do with her."

"But, Daddy, Sallie is sooooo tired of staying in there. She wants to help get money for poor children. Mommy could tie a ribbon on her for the handle. She has red nail polish to fix Sallie's chipped face too. Pleeeease, Daddy?"

CHAPTER 2
SALLIE IS SPRUCED UP

"Wow! Sallie looks beautiful, Mom!" Anna exclaimed when she arrived home from school the next day. You really fixed her up!"

"It didn't take long. She was a pretty little thing to begin with, and it was easy to spruce her up. Daddy took out the few dents she had," Anna's mother said as she held the small, shiny kettle in the air.

"See, I used a golden cord for her handle. I had some left over from the new curtains, and Daddy found bright red spray paint in the garage." Playfully she added, "You know, it would have taken a huge amount of nail polish to paint the whole kettle. It's a good thing your father had that can of paint. She does look wonderful, doesn't she?" Mother put Sallie back on the kitchen counter so she could finish making dinner.

"I love the way she looks." Anna thoughtfully picked up the kettle and twirled little Sallie around. She gently fingered the new handle.

"Daddy thinks she's too small to use outside at a store for Christmas. If we hang her up, the cord will break. Is there anything else we can do with her? She's so pretty. I want my friends to see her."

At dinner that night, the family discussion was all about little Sallie and what to do with her.

"She's too pretty to just sit here in the house."

"She's too small to hang on a big kettle stand."

"Too many coins might break her brand new handle."

"I could take her to school to show my friends."

After a few minutes, her mother's eyes grew wide and a smile crept across her face. "I have an idea! We can take her to your birthday party on Saturday. We can set her on the table so your friends can see her. Who knows, maybe someone will drop a few pennies in as they pass by. That will be a wonderful way for Sallie to help with Christmas."

CHAPTER 3
SALLIE GOES TO A BIRTHDAY PARTY

"Hey, Anna! This is a great party!" Oliver's mouth was full. He had a half-eaten piece of pizza in one hand and a glass of lemon-lime soda in the other.

He spotted the unusual table decoration and mumbled, "What's that bucket doing on the table?"

"She's not a bucket! Her name is Sallie Kettle."

"What's she for?" Oliver asked after gulping down a portion of the contents of his mouth.

"You put money in her."

"What for?"

"For poor children."

"Why?" His mouth was now empty except for the plastic drinking straw he was chasing around the rim of the glass.

"So they can have a nice Christmas if their parents don't have enough money."

Oliver finally caught up with the straw, took a sip, and yelled, "Mom, can I have some money for Sallie?"

Anna's mother heard Oliver talking to his mother, so she joined them to explain why they brought the kettle to the party. Oliver happily took the coins his mother gave him, dropped them into Sallie, and ran off to join the other children who were playing video games.

The other parents heard Anna's mother speaking about Sallie, so they gathered around to listen. Since all fifteen of the children at the party either went to the corps where Anna's parents were the corps officers, or were students at her charter school, their families were familiar with the tradition of the red kettle.

She told them how Anna and her father had rescued Sallie from the basement at the corps, and about Anna's conversation with the little kettle.

"Anna was certain that Sallie just couldn't stay in the bin another minute, and that there was something Sallie could do to help," her mother concluded.

"Was it Anna's idea to bring the smallest kettle out to fix it up and use it?" one parent asked.

"Yes. Anna wants so badly to help Sallie collect money, but we're not sure what the best solution is. The kettle is so small."

Another parent thought aloud, "I wonder what we could do this year to raise money for needy families, and use Sallie as the center attraction?"

That question was all it took to start a conversation about how Sallie could be used for Christmas.

"It's the beginning of December. We'll have to plan quickly," stated one parent.

"What about a bake sale?" asked another.

The questions and suggestions came faster and faster.

"A bake sale doesn't bring in much money."

"How does an indoor yard sale sound? We could put tables in the youth room at the corps."

"I'm not sure how we could get enough items to sell on such short notice, and the youth room is not that big."

As they were talking, someone suggested they take notes to remember what was said.

"What if we passed Sallie from room to room at school and the children could bring in their loose change? Oh, wait! That's OUR loose change, not the children's. Besides, that won't generate enough money to help even one family."

"Those gift-trees in malls are a good idea. You know, the ones with children's names hung on them, but there's not enough time to set that up."

"What if each classroom adopts a family in need?"

"That still puts the financial burden on just the families at school. It would be great to have lots of other people involved in this project. How could we get more people to join us?"

"Maybe our thinking is too narrow. Let's start thinking in bigger terms."

The parents decided they wanted a plan that would help as many families as possible. They all agreed that baked goods and an indoor yard sale would not be nearly enough.

As their excitement grew, the parents came up with a wonderful plan.

"How about giving each class at school the opportunity to choose a project? We can have a "Christmas Faire."

"Let's have it in the gym at the corps and invite the Sunday school classes to join in. Each class can have a table or floor space for their activity."

"We could advertise and invite the community to support the fund-raiser and have family fun at the same time."

"That's great! I think this will work. I can organize advertising in the newspaper and on the radio."

"I'll send e-mails to other churches and service clubs in town, so they can advertise to their members."

"I'll cover the other schools. I'll e-mail flyers they can print and send home with their students. Can we add this announcement to the corps' web page?"

"Let's make a list of possible activities we could offer so we can include them in the advertisements."

The parents continued to brainstorm while their children played. The activity list for the faire was lengthy, and included many different categories from which the students and teachers could choose. One father wisely reminded everyone that this venture would require approval from several people. Since Anna's father had already given his consent to use the corps gymnasium, it was just a matter of securing approval from the principal and the charter school's advisory panel.

CHAPTER 4
SALLIE IS NEARLY FORGOTTEN

Two weeks after Anna's birthday party, the Christmas Faire preparations were nearly finished. Mr. Higgins, the school principal, had immediately given his hearty approval when he heard the plan, as did the school advisory panel.

It was amazing how excited all the teachers were about the faire. They and their students came up with even more suggestions than the parents had thought of at Anna's birthday party.

Mrs. Thurston's third-grade class asked Mr. Thurston to take family portraits of the shoppers at the faire. The students painted two white sheets as backdrops so families could choose a winter scene with a snowman, or a cozy fireplace with a decorated tree.

Mr. Thurston offered to print the pictures on the spot, and put them in 5x7 frames, too.

The children in Miss Fisher's fourth-grade class wrote Christmas stories, printed ten copies of each one, and took them to Mr. Webber's print shop to have them assembled into books. Each child drew a unique cover, which Mr. Webber copied and stapled to the children's stories. These would be sold at their bake sale table along with all the goodies their parents agreed to make.

The music teacher arranged for a brass quartette to play and eight vocalists to sing Christmas carols the entire day of the faire. They even agreed to dress in winter Victorian costumes. He also asked the local radio talk show host to auction off the larger items that had been donated.

The adult Sunday school class promised to organize the donated clothing and food for easy distribution, and the Young Peoples' Singing Company agreed to join with the sixth grade choir for lunchtime entertainment.

Everything was ready the night before the faire. The students had finished decorating the Christmas tree in the center of the gym. The clothing drive and food collection tables were near the door to the parking lot for easy access, and one basketball hoop was lowered for the bean bag toss. Everything was in place when the principal and Anna's father plugged in the football and air hockey games, exhaled, and congratulated each other on a job well done.

"I think we're ready, Major."

"I believe so, Dave, and we still have time for dinner with our families. I'll come back later to finish the decorations around the tree. It's a one-man job. Won't take me long. Thanks for your help! See you tomorrow."

In spite of all the excitement, Anna appeared troubled when her father came home. He noticed the concerned look on her face when they sat down for dinner and asked, "What's the matter, Anna? Are you worried about something?"

Anna began to cry. "We've had so much fun getting ready for the faire. I've drawn my pictures and made tree ornaments, but no one's thought about Sallie! There's no place for her. The gym will be full of tables and people! There's no room left," she sobbed.

Her father held out his arms to her for a hug. Anna jumped from her chair and ran to him. "I have a very special place reserved for Sallie," he told her as his strong arms folded warmly around her. "Don't worry, sweetie. I haven't forgotten how this adventure started."

CHAPTER 5
SALLIE IS THE STAR

Anna was breathless when she saw the small kettle the next morning in the gym. "Oh, Daddy, Sallie's beautiful! You didn't forget her!"

Anna's father had made a miniature kettle stand and Sallie was suspended by her new gold cord handle. He had put her on a tall, narrow table with a yellow cloth beside the Christmas tree. A spotlight from the ceiling gave Sallie a brilliant shine that made her sparkle more brightly than ever.

Sallie was the center of attention all day long at the Christmas Faire, and at noon, just before the sixth-grade choir joined the Y. P. Singing Company to sing, and sloppy joes and hot dogs were served, Anna's father stood by the tree in the middle of the gymnasium to give a little speech.

"Thank you all for coming today. I know you'll continue to have a great time. Thanks, too, for helping to make Christmas a little happier for needy families in our community.

"I'm glad that our congregation was happy to join the charter school students and teachers to make this fun day happen." This all started with the tender heart of a six-year-old, who heard the cries of a little one who was left alone in the dark.

"From that beginning, a desire grew among parents to continue the spirit of giving during this Christmas season. That's why we have enjoyed this wonderful faire today. And we've already emptied the coins from Sallie eleven times!"

Cheers and loud clapping erupted from parents and students alike at this announcement.

"With those coins, and the games and sales, we have raised enough money, just this morning, to help six families."

He continued with a twinkle in his eye. "So, our heartfelt thanks go to Anna, for listening carefully enough to hear little Sallie Kettle, to the parents who caught the vision to help others, and to the teachers, the students and their parents, and the Sunday school classes who planned this faire."

The applause and cheers were so loud and lasted for such a long time that Anna hid her face behind her mother's Victorian skirt and covered her ears.

After the cheers died down, her father continued, "So, listen to the choir, enjoy your lunch, and have lots of fun!"

Anna's father and the school principal were the last to leave the corps when the festivities were finished.

After sweeping the gymnasium floor, they sat for a few minutes with their feet up on folding chairs. "Thanks for your help, Dave," Anna's father said. "This would not have taken place without you."

"This really was great fun, Major. Lots of work involved, but the results are extremely satisfying. It looks like we have more than enough food, clothing, and new toys to help at least twenty families. I'm sure the money we raised will go a long way to make Christmas especially wonderful for many more families.

"It was a great idea to make this a community event, instead of just depending on the students' families to support it. Who would have thought we could have such success with one simple idea?"

The Major replied, "My grandmother Crissinger always said, 'Little is much when it's given to God.' I think the success today proves that." With that said, they got up to leave and turned out the lights.

They both were so tired that neither of them realized the spotlight over little Sallie Kettle was still on

EPILOGUE

When the Christmas Eve candlelight service was finished at the corps, Anna and her father took Sallie from her place of honor near the chapel door to put her in the basement bin with the rest of Sallie's kettle family.

A big yawn got in her way as Anna thanked her father for letting Sallie help at the Christmas Faire. "You and Sallie helped quite a few families have a wonderful Christmas they'll remember for a long time."

"I'm glad my friends helped too," she mumbled as another yawn started to form.

Anna noticed that the small kettle's eyes were already closed, so she gently set Sallie down in the bin, being careful not to wake her. She patted the little kettle and said, "Nightie-night, Sallie."

Sallie smiled sleepily, without opening her eyes, and in a soft voice, whispered, "That was fun, Anna. Remember me for next year…" z z z z

ABOUT THE AUTHOR

Major Deborah L. Cranford, MA, along with her husband, Paul, served for twenty-five years as Salvation Army officers. They have three children and five grandchildren. Deborah is the author of several Bible studies relating to recovery issues, and has been recognized for her writing ability. Debbi and Paul maintain a retirement home in Myrtle Beach, South Carolina, and enjoy traveling, reading, and music.

THANK YOU...

…to Commissioner Israel L. Gaither for his kind words.

…to Commissioner James M. Knaggs for his practical support.

…to Majors John and Judy Cheydleur for their literary and technical wisdom.

…to our new friend, Michael Cormier, for capturing on paper what was in my head.

…to Major Virginia Van Brunt for her newly discovered gift of salesmanship.

www.ingramcontent.com/pod-product-compliance
Lightning Source LLC
Chambersburg PA
CBRC090840010526
44119CB00044B/498